★ Government in ★
Your City or Town

Karen Kenney

rourkeeducationalmedia.com

Scan for Related Titles and Teacher Resources

Before Reading:

Building Academic Vocabulary and Background Knowledge

Before reading a book, it is important to tap into what your child or students already know about the topic. This will help them develop their vocabulary, increase their reading comprehension, and make connections across the curriculum.

1. *Look at the cover of the book. What will this book be about?*
2. *What do you already know about the topic?*
3. *Let's study the Table of Contents. What will you learn about in the book's chapters?*
4. *What would you like to learn about this topic? Do you think you might learn about it from this book? Why or why not?*
5. *Use a reading journal to write about your knowledge of this topic. Record what you already know about the topic and what you hope to learn about the topic.*
6. *Read the book.*
7. *In your reading journal, record what you learned about the topic and your response to the book.*
8. *After reading the book complete the activities below.*

Content Area Vocabulary
Read the list. What do these words mean?

amendment
budget
constitution
executive
federalist
governs
grant
independent
judicial
legislative
limited
services

After Reading:

Comprehension and Extension Activity

After reading the book, work on the following questions with your child or students in order to check their level of reading comprehension and content mastery.

1. *What would happen if a town or city's budget ran out? (Infer)*
2. *What does it mean to have limited powers in local governments? (Summarize)*
3. *What did the Nineteenth Amendment do? (Summarize)*
4. *What would your town look like if important services were no longer available? (Asking questions)*
5. *Who elects the mayor? (Summarize)*

Extension Activity

Think about all the services in your town. What does each service do? Why are these services important? Your town has reached its budget and is deciding to cut one of the many services including police, fire, public transportation, sanitation department, and public works. You must rally with your community to save these services by writing a letter to the mayor explaining the importance of these departments. State how these departments serve your community's basic needs and what would happen if they were removed.

Table of Contents

What Is a City or Town Government?

A fire rages in the house next door. In minutes, a fire engine arrives. Firefighters extinguish the blaze, and your neighborhood is safe again. A fire department is a vital service in any town or city. The area's government runs this and other important community **services**.

A local government makes the area it **governs** a good place to live by keeping it clean and safe. It also enforces the laws made by the state government.

Cleaning the streets and building parks are some things a local government manages in a city or town.

The United States became an **independent** nation in 1776. The U.S. Constitution set the rules for a new government. It created a **federalist** government. This means the country's powers are split between states and the national government.

The nation's leaders signed the U.S. Constitution on September 17, 1787.

The states then set up local governments. The local governments had to follow rules set by the state and the country.

Local Government's Role

All cities and towns have some basic needs. The roads need to be cleaned and plowed. Streets need to have signs posted or have traffic lights installed. Public buses and trains need to transport people around the area. Drinking water must be clean and garbage needs to be taken from homes.

Government workers plow snow from public roads.

Important services like police and fire departments are also necessary when running a city or town. These are all some of the much needed services that local governments provide.

Police make sure that laws are obeyed.

All cities and towns have different needs. The government provides services needed in its community. A town or city government uses a **budget** to fund its departments and boards. It also monitors how well each one works. Some towns or cities need better ways to recycle garbage. Some need to find new ways to run their schools. Other towns or cities need to use more money to fix roads.

Local governments have **limited** powers. The state government must **grant** them their powers. This means that cities and towns must follow the state's **constitution**.

Local governments do not have as much power as state governments.

★ Forms of Local Government ★

Power is balanced in a local government. It is organized much like the federal and state governments. No branch of the government has too much power. Mayors lead the **executive** branch. City councils or other groups run the **legislative** branch. Cities and towns also have local courts. They make up the **judicial** branch.

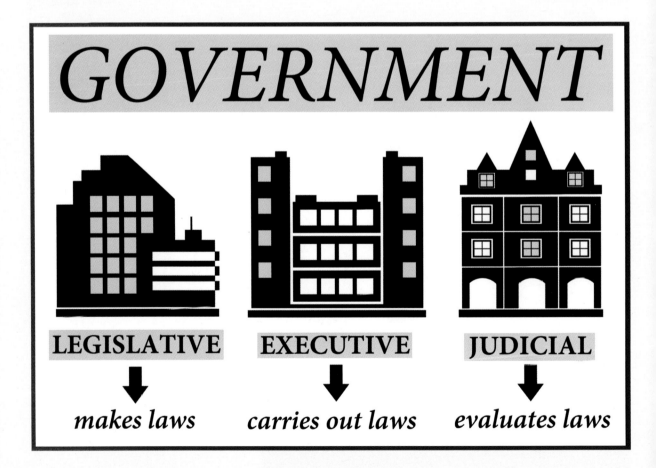

GOVERNMENT

LEGISLATIVE → *makes laws*

EXECUTIVE → *carries out laws*

JUDICIAL → *evaluates laws*

Mayor-Council Government

There are three main forms of local government. The mayor-council form is the oldest in the United States. People living in the city or town elect their mayor. Council members are sometimes elected. Or the mayor may appoint the council members. The mayor or the council chooses department heads. The departments run different services, such as a fire department.

Strong Mayor Model

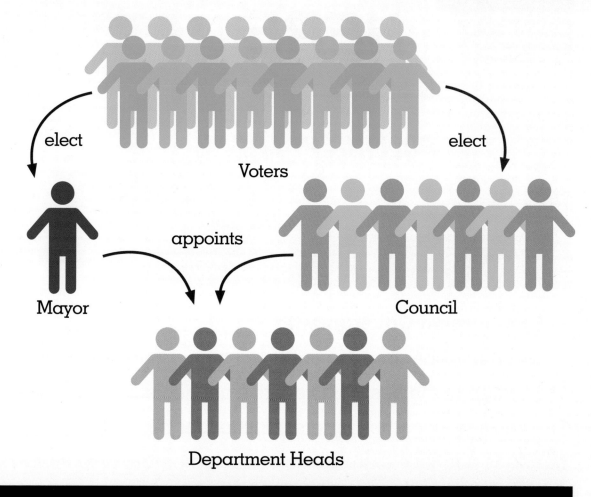

elect

Voters

elect

appoints

Mayor

Council

Department Heads

This chart shows how a strong mayor-council city government is formed.

Voters elect their town leaders during an election.

Commission Government

A commission government is led by a group of leaders. This group combines the executive and legislative branches. The citizens elect the leaders. One leader heads the group but does not have extra powers. Each member also heads a department. Commissions have three to seven members.

In 2012, there were 19,522 city or town governments in the United States.

Many city governments are run from the city hall.

Council-Manager Government

A council-manager government has an elected council. It also has a mayor. The mayor has little power in making laws in this type of government. Instead, the council makes the laws. The council also hires a manager. This manager advises the council and leads the government's staff.

Famous Mayors

Some city mayors have made a great impact on their cities. Fiorello LaGuardia was New York City's mayor from 1934 to 1945. He used his time in office to clean up the city. He improved the fire and police departments. He built playgrounds and health clinics. He also made laws to crack down on gangs and crime in the city.

New York City is the largest city in the United States.

Fiorello LaGuardia
1882–1947

LaGuardia had a weekly radio show while in office. During a newspaper strike in 1945 he read aloud the daily comic strips. He did not want New York City's children to miss reading their favorite comics, like *Dick Tracy* and *Little Orphan Annie*.

Susanna Salter
1860–1961

In June 1919, the Nineteenth **Amendment** passed, giving women the right to vote. Just a few months later, Susanna Salter became the first female city mayor. She was elected mayor of Argonia, Kansas in April 1887.

Carl Stokes made history when he became the first African American city mayor in 1967. He was the mayor of Cleveland, Ohio.

Carl Stokes was Cleveland's mayor from 1968 to 1971.

Local governments work to keep towns and cities safe, clean, and fun places to live. They manage important services, like the police department. They build playgrounds and parks. They make sure garbage is taken away and the water is cleaned.

A local government makes sure kids have fun and safe places to play.

Have you been to the park lately? Take a look around. It is pretty, safe, and clean because of your local government.

Glossary

amendment (uh-MEND-muhnt): change or addition to a legal document

budget (BUHJ-it): a plan for how to earn and spend money

constitution (kon-stuh-TOO-shuhn): the system of laws in a state or a country that outline personal rights and ways to govern

executive (eg-ZEK-yuh-tiv): a branch of government that effects the laws of a state or country

federalist (FED-ur-uhl-ist): a country that has both national and state governments and shares powers

governs (GUHV-urnz): controls a town or city using laws

grant (grant): to agree to give something

independent (in-di-PEN-duhnt): not controlled by someone else

judicial (joo-DISH-uhl): a branch of government that deals with enforcing laws and a state or country's courts

legislative (LEJ-iss-lay-tiv): a branch of government that makes or changes laws

limited (LIM-i-tid): small or restricted

services (SUR-viss-iz): systems that provide things that are useful or needed

Index

Show What You Know

1. What are the three forms of a city or town government?
2. What services do local governments control?
3. Who was Fiorello LaGuardia?
4. Why might a person want to be mayor?
5. How has your local government helped you?

Websites to Visit

bensguide.gpo.gov/3-5/index.html
kidscorner.org/html/halloffame03.php
www.cccoe.net/govern

About the Author

Karen Latchana Kenney is the author of more than 80 books for children. She's written about many forms of government and U.S. symbols, like the White House and the American bald eagle. Kenney lives in Minneapolis, Minnesota.

Meet The Author!
www.meetREMauthors.com

PHOTO CREDITS: Cover/ Title Page © Trekandshoot; page 4 © MarkCoffeyPhoto; page 5 © KingWu; page 6 © U.S. National Archives and Record Administration; page 7 © Ken Wiedermann; page 8 © Martine Oger; page 9 © Pamela Joe McFarlane; page 10 © montiannoowong; page 11 © phillyskater; page 12 © icefields; page 13 © Blankstock; page 14 © YinYang; page 15 © Michael Guttman; page 16 © mamahoohooba; page 17 © Library of Congress; page 18 © Kansas Historical Society/Wikipedia; page 19 © Brian Busovicki 2008; page 20 © Xuguang Wang/XenGate; page 21 © Monkey Business Images

Edited by: Jill Sherman

Cover by: Nicola Stratford, nicolastratford.com
Interior design by: Jen Thomas

Library of Congress PCN Data

Government in Your City or Town/ Karen Kenney
(U.S. Government and Civics)
ISBN 978-1-62717-684-2 (hard cover)
ISBN 978-1-62717-806-8 (soft cover)
ISBN 978-1-62717-922-5 (e-Book)
Library of Congress Control Number: 2014935460

Printed in the United States of America, North Mankato, Minnesota

Also Available as: